YOUR KNOWLEDGE HAS VALUE

- We will publish your bachelor's and master's thesis, essays and papers

- Your own eBook and book - sold worldwide in all relevant shops

- Earn money with each sale

Upload your text at www.GRIN.com and publish for free

Bibliographic information published by the German National Library:

The German National Library lists this publication in the National Bibliography; detailed bibliographic data are available on the Internet at http://dnb.dnb.de .

This book is copyright material and must not be copied, reproduced, transferred, distributed, leased, licensed or publicly performed or used in any way except as specifically permitted in writing by the publishers, as allowed under the terms and conditions under which it was purchased or as strictly permitted by applicable copyright law. Any unauthorized distribution or use of this text may be a direct infringement of the author s and publisher s rights and those responsible may be liable in law accordingly.

Imprint:

Copyright © 2018 GRIN Verlag
Print and binding: Books on Demand GmbH, Norderstedt Germany
ISBN: 9783668688377

This book at GRIN:

https://www.grin.com/document/421202

Sebastian Moritz

High Frequency Trading. Its effects on stock markets and how to control them

GRIN Verlag

GRIN - Your knowledge has value

Since its foundation in 1998, GRIN has specialized in publishing academic texts by students, college teachers and other academics as e-book and printed book. The website www.grin.com is an ideal platform for presenting term papers, final papers, scientific essays, dissertations and specialist books.

Visit us on the internet:

http://www.grin.com/

http://www.facebook.com/grincom

http://www.twitter.com/grin_com

Title: High Frequency Trading: Its effects on stock markets and how to control them

Sebastian Moritz

Fremdsprache Studienzweig 6 (Englisch)

Hochschule Harz – University of Applied Sciences

Winter Semester 2017/ 2018

Not long ago the worlds' stock markets looked like this: Big rooms with walls covered by monitors showing continuously changing graphs, numbers, and columns. In the room, on the floor, a nervous crowd of traders and brokers shouting in a muddle, trying to buy and sell stocks. This picture has changed- we are still able to observe the room and the monitors, just the hectic crowd of traders has shrunken together. Quietly working computers have taken over its place. (World Economy, 2014) The computers process information faster, never take time off and in fact, rarely need somebody to control them. (Seith, 2010) Some of these high-frequency trading (HFT) computers are stocked with customized trading programs. These programs known as algorithms are based on mathematical formulas. They are able to independently evaluate stock market rates and to pursue complex strategies at a clearly faster pace than human traders ever could. (World Economy, 2014) "The high-frequency traders' basic strategy is very simple: trade as much and as quickly as possible. The profit margin on each transaction is frequently quite small, but these small amounts add up to billions due to mass and velocity." (World Economy, 2014) This strategy only pays off, if the trading programs are always a split second faster than everyone else. Therefore, the distance to the stock market plays a key role, since it's about millionth seconds. The shorter the cable, the faster the fluency of information. (Bonometti, 2014) While high frequency-traders represent only a small part of all traders, approximately 60% of all US stock trades and 40% of all EU stock trades can be accredited to them. (Seith, 2010) Even though many market researchers state that they increase the market's liquidity and decrease volatility, the incredible speed, the scale and the non-transparent way in which the high-speed traders operate raise skepticism among market-observers worldwide. The fear of market manipulation and conventional controlling systems losing grasp has grown. Those fears found confirmation on "Black Thursday 2.0" (Seith, 2010) when in May 2010 the first so-called flash crash, caused by an uncontrolled rampage of several, interacting algorithms, made Dow Jones collapse out of thin air. (Buchter, 2014) First regulatory steps have been implemented to prevent such incidents in future. HFT might bring some benefits for stock markets such as higher liquidity and the reduction of volatility, but there are dangerous risks such as the systematic bypassing of conventional traders, market manipulation and technical errors. Hence it is essential to implement further regulatory measurements to control HFT for the sake of equity, integrity and stability of global stock markets.

At latest when the 1st flash crash happened at Wall Street back in 2010, when a market value of almost $1 trillion disappeared within only minutes (Heismann, 2013), the advantages and disadvantages of HFT are being discussed forcefully and make the whole topic strongly controversial. Proponents claim that "HFT [...][is not] harmful [...],but [...] creates additional liquidity [...][for the market]" (Reimer, 2012). If a market has a high level of liquidity that means that a recipient can be found for every offer made. (World Economy, 2014). Proponents claim that this is especially important now, that many traders move away from official trading platforms to alternative non-transparent private platforms, so-called Dark Pools. (Heismann, 2013) Attached to this circumstance is the fear of decreasing liquidity on official trading platforms. However, "the liquidity created by HFT is extremely fleeting" says Hans Burg, professor of banking business at the University of Hohenheim. Further, high-frequency traders work especially efficient in markets that are highly liquid already, since they are dependent on purchasers for their high volume deals. High-frequency traders also see themselves accused that they retreat in case of crises when liquidity is needed most. (Nagel, 2016) ETH Zürich researchers declared in a study from 2012: "We question in particular the argument that HFT provides liquidity and suggest that the welfare gains derived from HFT are minimal and perhaps even largely negative on a long-term investment horizon." (Henn, 2013) Another claim made is that HFT is decreasing the volatility on conventional stock markets. (O'Brien, 2014) This means that the fluctuation of stock prices between different locations and in general decreases, what improves price quality and fairness (Francioni, 2012). The assertion is highly controversial though since there is dissent, on how to measure the effect (Neill, 2012) because some trading algorithms have the opposite effect. (deutsche-boerse.com, 2013).

Opponents fear tremendous disadvantages and an increased disparity for traders who cannot afford the programming of an HFT algorithm or its installation. (Nagel, 2016)The programming of an HFT algorithm is quite costly which makes it inaccessible for traders who lack the required purchasing power. Same counts for the computers needed. Successful high-frequency traders need the fastest computers available on the market since those machines need to place millions of orders per day. Experts assume that only during the rush hour at Wall Street between 3 pm and 4 pm each one of those machines trades volumes up to 80 million securities. (Welchering, 2012) For this endeavor a machine is needed that is at least ranked in the top 20 of the fastest computers worldwide. The purchasing price for these high-performance computers is $50 to $60 million. On top, there are estimated running costs of $7.5 million, annually. (Welchering, 2012). Since it is all about speed, it is necessary to place the machines close to the stock market. Many high-frequency traders take advantage of so-called co-location services. (Bonometti, 2014) These are rental services offered by the stock markets themselves, which allow high-frequency traders to place their computers literally in the same building as the stock markets servers, in exchange for a costly fee. (Picardo, 2016) These special machine placements enable high-frequency traders to directly tap the main artery of financial information and to process them in the fastest way possible. (Buchter, 2014) This obvious financial barrier excludes normal traders from accessing the technology and significantly improves the competitive position of those can access it. (Bonometti, 2014)

The advantage high-frequency traders get for their investment is a clear information edge and the resulting ability to react in a speed which normal traders cannot match. (Buchter, 2014) In an interview in December 2012, Andrew Brooks described high-frequency traders as: "[Gamblers who] can see the end of a horse race and then place bets on the winning horse." (Henn, 2013) There are two main tactics high-frequency traders can pursue to make use of their information edge. The first tactic is the so-called "rebate arbitrage" (Picardo, 2016) They can spot price trends before anybody else does. Hence, they are enabled to buy stocks of an in value increasing commodity and resell it to slower traders, milliseconds later, before the price trend has ended, with a minimal profit per share. Similar to black market dealers, they buy the good tickets before anybody else can buy them and then sell them more expensively later. (Buchter, 2014) This has the effect that slower traders do not only pay an explicit exchange fee, "but also an implicit fee for high-frequency trading, because this type of trading is interposed between most stock market transactions" (World Economy, 2014) The second tactic is the so-called "front running". (Nagel, 2016) This tactic allows high-frequency traders to make profits with almost no risks. A big institutional trader (T1), for instance, sends out an order for 10,000 shares of a commodity (C1) offering $X per share. Due to its superior speed, the HFT algorithm can process that information, buy all available shares of C1 and then to sell them to T1 for a price of $X+1. (O'Brien, 2014) The resell price only differs by a minimum cent amount per share but summed up this intermediate tradeoff results in significantly higher costs for the conventional trader T1. (Bonometti, 2014) Both scenarios improve liquidity illusionary, but in fact, only outsmart the "slower" conventional traders, by causing higher costs to them. (Nagel, 2016)

It is difficult and costly to always be a step ahead, especially since many different high-frequency algorithms face competition against each other. In his book 'Flash Boys' Michael Lewis explicitly describes how an HFT company installs fiber optic cables between Chicago and New York, spending $300 million, to only save three milliseconds. (O'Brien, 2014) Opponents of HFT claim that it is a common practice to manipulate the market to slow down and deceive the competition instead. The tactics used by HFT here can be seen as stout manipulation of the market. (Sethi, 2014) As NBA coaching Legend Red Auerbach once put it: "[If you want to] gain a competitive edge, [...] you cheat". There are two main tactics used by algo-traders to slow down competitors and to shape conditions in their favor. The first one to mention is the so-called 'Quote stuffing'. Here an HFT algorithm is quickly entering and withdrawing large amounts of unimportant orders to flood the market with irrelevant quotes that competitors have to process. (www.investopedia.com) The time required by competitor programs to process the useless information is costing them valuable milliseconds and is so eliminating their competitive edge. (Hell, 2013) The spreading of too many quotes at once is believed to have been one reason for the flash crash in 2010 according to investigations of the US stock analysis company Nanex. (Nanex, 2010) The second manipulation technique to name is so-called "spoofing". Here a trading program places a number of overpriced purchase offers. The extreme operational speed allows the HFT program to cancel these offers before anybody can respond to them. (Stinson, 2013) Nevertheless, these illusionary offers are seen. The illusion that some traders are willing to buy the offers and that the price will rise, is created. Other trader's reaction to this illusion does then, in fact, raise the price. (World Economy, 2014) Previously bought stocks, acquired to a regular price can now be sold profitably. (www.nanex.net, 2013) Both cases represent significant interferences into trade through superior technological advances. (Matthews, 2012) They create no additional value for the market itself. Instead they even absorb value and take it away, fully automatically and with calculated precision.

This automated precision comes along with the risk of technical failure. The more sophisticated the competition gets, the more code is needed, the more programs are built, the more problems occur according to Lewis Lesokhin, CTO of CAST. "The systems are getting too complex for any of the brilliant developers they have building them to manage them". (Lesokhin, 2014) With the increasing complexity of those algorithms the risk of inherent coding errors increases significantly. The list of algorithm malfunctions recorded with dramatic effects on the market is long. To name a few: (19. August 2013) Everbright Securities, accidentally buys shares for $3.8 billion, in Shanghai, which makes the stock market rise by 5.6% within seconds. (20. August 2013) Goldman Sachs accidentally buys a high volume of stocks with names alphabetically sorted starting from H to L, losing $100 million and causing major confusion at Wall Street. (2. August 2012) Knight Capital introduces parts of new code which accidentally reactivate old parts of the code and start havoc. Knight Capital loses $440 million within 30 minutes, has to be taken over by Getco and causes the worst flash crash for Wall Street since May 2010. (Hofstetter, 2013) Another variation of algorithm failure occurs when various trading programs repeatedly react to one another and so get caught in a loop. (World Economy, 2014) The speed in which this happens is too fast for human traders to intervene and could only be tracked and stopped by special programs. (Buchter, 2014) However, errors and technical loops like this are believed to be a crucial factor for suddenly occurring flash crashes at global stock markets. (Matthews, 2012) This problem is still present, research conducted by CNN connotes that at least a dozen of mini flash crashes happens on a daily basis. (Farrell, 2013) The crux is that an error occurring in the digital world has sensible effects on real economies, real companies, and real people.

The disadvantages for many institutional traders and the risk of manipulation are unfavorable for a large majority of market participants, while code errors can have a damaging impact on economy. The benefits are meanwhile devastatingly exploited by a relatively small group of high-frequency traders. Further, the stability of conventional stock exchanges is endangered since conventional human traders may more and more retreat into dark pools knowing they cannot at all compete with the algo-traders competitive advantages. (O'Brien, 2014) Even Ex-Goldman Sachs Chairman Gary Cohn recently warned in an interview with Wall Street Journal that the industry must become conscious of those HFT activities, which strain the market in a way, it's infrastructure is not made for (Buchter, 2014)

Seeing that conventional control mechanisms couldn't keep pace with the high-frequency technology, stock markets and governments took first steps in order to counter these problems. (Hofstetter, 2013) There are regulations such as MiFID (Markets in Financial Instruments Directive) set up and adopted by the European Union as first legal regulations and restrictions in spring 2014. (Heldt, 2014) Further regulations will presumably be implemented in January 2018 with the MiFID II norms. One regulatory measurement, introduced with MiFID and standard at most stock exchanges as well, was the so-called circuit breaker mechanism. If volatility crosses certain boundaries, trading will automatically be stopped. This doesn't completely stop flash crashes from happening, but it can minimize their effects and damages to a tolerable level. (Heismann, 2013) Another regulation introduced was the increase of the so-called "tick size". The tick size is the minimum by which a market price can change. Since price changes occur less frequently through that, it represents an indirect regulation of HFT. (World Economy, 2014) In Germany, trades conducted by HFT must further be tagged by stock exchanges. (section 16 (2) no. 3 of the German Stock Exchange Act (Börsengesetz – BörsG) (www.bafin.de, 2014). Additional regulations have been made, which are not binding for the stock exchanges and could voluntarily be implemented. Firstly, stock markets have been asked not constrained to prevent the occurrence of mass phantom quotes, which would prevent quote stuffing. (tagesspiegel.de, 2013) Secondly "the stock markets are being directed to make privileged electronic connections to stock exchange computers fair and transparent for all market participants" (World Economy, 2014).That would mean the elimination of co-locations, which puts stock markets in a conflict of interest since they considerably profit of those. In consequence, the implementation is pretty unlikely, and possibilities for manipulation remain.

To effectively abandon these grey areas in which HFT programs can still operate the following regulations would be conceivable. -The introduction of a limit for offer cancellations. Through this especially tactics such as spoofing would lose their basis of existence. (World Economy, 2014) -The introduction of a minimum holding period, as proposed by the European Parliament. (tagesspiegel.de, 2013) This would mean that any stock acquired must be kept for a certain period, before it can be re-sold (500 milliseconds in case of the EU Parliaments proposal) Due to a mechanism like that, manipulation techniques such as front-running would be eliminated entirely. Also, the risk of flash crashes would decrease. (World Economy, 2014) Another approach that is forcefully discussed quite recently would be the charge of a financial transaction tax. Paul Krugman argues: "we need a financial transactions tax—something like 0.1 percent on all trades—to make this kind of socially useless speculation personally useless too. Long-term investors wouldn't notice this small tax, but ultra-short-term investors would: their warp speed trading would become less profitable and less prevalent." (O'Brien, 2014) It is further possible to counter the problem through from the technological side. Brad Katsuyama created the stock exchange platform IEX, which uses special signal interruption technologies. (Bonometti, 2014) Hence, "A traditional trader can't be outrun by high-frequency traders" (Katsuyama, 2014). But this is by far not the global standard.

What this all amounts to is that high-frequency-trading exhibits significantly more points of criticism than positive aspects. The actual behavior of HFT algorithms in its extreme form is not generating any additional value for the economy, but solely for the HFT investors. Often through systematic and targeted deception of slower, weaker market participants. (Hell, 2013) The solution for sure is not, to eliminate algo-trading entirely, but to restrict its extreme forms to prevent harm to society. It is therefore important that the technological progress is accompanied by the creation of an appropriate legislative and technological infrastructure through governments and stock exchange platforms. (World

Economy, 2014) HFT can so merit its suitable role within the market structure, but should not in any way be able to burden or to damage it. (Nagel, 2016) Equity, integrity and stability of global stock markets would be restored. The question left open, is whether humans cause more harm when they write algorithms or when they trade on their own. (Neill, 2012)

List of references

Bonometti, B. (2014, October 14). *www.srf.ch*. Retrieved December 6, 2017, from https://www.srf.ch/news/wirtschaft/millionen-in-millisekunden

Borger, J., Goossens, H., Schutgens, Marie (Producers), & Meerman, M. (Director). (2013). *The Wall Steet Code* [Motion Picture]. USA: You Tube.

Buchter, H. (2014, April 10). *www.zeit.de*. Retrieved December 4, 2017, from http://www.zeit.de/2014/16/hochfrequenzhandel-algorithmen-boerse/seite-2

deutsche-boerse.com. (2013). Retrieved December 6, 2017, from http://deutsche-boerse.com/dbg-de/ueber-uns/public-affairs/aktuelle-themen/hochfrequenzhandel

Dr.Nagel, J. (2016, April 30). *www.bundesbank.de*. Retrieved December 5, 2017, from https://www.bundesbank.de/Redaktion/DE/Reden/2012/2012_07_04_nagel_hft_und_martkimplikationen.html

Farrell, M. (2013, March 20). *money.cnn.com*. Retrieved December 9, 2017, from http://money.cnn.com/2013/03/20/investing/mini-flash-crash

Francioni, R. (2012, September 6). Hochfrequenzhandel und Börse. *Frankfurter Allgemeine Zeitung*, 19.

Heismann, G. (2013, November 13). *www.wiwo.de*. (W. Woche, Editor) Retrieved Dezember 5, 2017, from http://www.wiwo.de/finanzen/boerse/dark-pools-dark-pools-verlangen-geringere-gebuehren/9082884-2.html

Heldt, D. C. (2014). *www.wirtschaftslexikon.gabler.der*. (S. G. Verlag, Editor) Retrieved December 11, 2017, from http://wirtschaftslexikon.gabler.de/Archiv/56953/mifid-v9.html

Hell, S. (2013, December 18). *www.wallstreet-online.de*. Retrieved December 8, 2017, from https://www.wallstreet-online.de/nachricht/6471482-high-frequency-trading-hft-teil-7-quote-stuffing-15-000-orders-3-sekunden

Henn, M. (2013, March). *www.weed-online.org*. Retrieved December 7, 2017, from http://www2.weed-online.org/uploads/factsheet_high_frequency_trading.pdf

Hofstetter, Y. (2013, October 15). *www.faz.net*. Retrieved December 9, 2017, from http://www.faz.net/aktuell/feuilleton/risiken-des-hochfrequenzhandels-das-systemische-risiko-der-dummheit-12619019-p2.html

Krugman, P. (2009, November 26). *www.nytimes.com*. Retrieved December 11, 2017, from http://www.nytimes.com/2009/11/27/opinion/27krugman.html

Lesokhin, L. (2014, May 31). There's Another Big Issue With High-Frequency Trading That Hardly Anyone Is Talking About. (L. Lopez, Interviewer, & B. Insider, Editor) United States of America.

Matthews, C. (2012, August 8). *business.time.com*. Retrieved December 9, 2017, from http://business.time.com/2012/08/08/high-frequency-trading-wall-streets-doomsday-machine/

Nanex. (2010, May 6). *www.nanex.net*. Retrieved December 8, 2017, from http://www.nanex.net/FlashCrash/FlashCrashAnalysis_QuoteLife.html

Neill, G. (2012, 2 25). *www.economist.com*. Retrieved December 6, 2017, from http://www.economist.com/node/21547988

O'Brien, M. (2014, April 11). *www.theatlantic.com*. Retrieved December 8, 2017, from https://www.theatlantic.com/business/archive/2014/04/everything-you-need-to-know-about-high-frequency-trading/360411/

O'Brien, M. (2014, February 2014). *www.theatlantic.com*. Retrieved December 8, 2017, from https://www.theatlantic.com/business/archive/2014/02/high-speed-trading-isnt-about-efficiency-its-about-cheating/283677/

Picardo, E. (2016, August 5). *www.investopedia.com*. Retrieved December 7, 2017, from https://www.investopedia.com/articles/active-trading/042414/youd-better-know-your-highfrequency-trading-terminology.asp

Reimer, H. (2012, August 29). *www.wiwo.de*. (W. Woche, Ed.) Retrieved December 5, 2017, from http://www.wiwo.de/finanzen/boerse/boersenkenner-rudolf-ferscha-liquiditaet-schuetzen/7049278.html

Seith, A. (2010, September 27). *www.spiegel.de*. Retrieved December 3, 2017, from http://www.spiegel.de/wirtschaft/unternehmen/automatischer-boersenhandel-turbocomputer-mischen-aktienmaerkte-auf-a-719085.html

Sethi, R. (2014, April 6). *blogspot.de*. Retrieved December 8, 2017, from http://rajivsethi.blogspot.de/2014/04/superfluous-financial-intermediation.html?spref=tw

Stinson, L. (2013, July 30). *www.lexology.com*. Retrieved December 8, 2017, from https://www.lexology.com/library/detail.aspx?g=c6f66fb4-e220-47be-896a-7352984c9622

tagesspiegel.de. (2013, February 28). Retrieved December 11, 2017, from http://www.tagesspiegel.de/wirtschaft/finanzmaerkte-bundestag-beschliesst-gesetz-gegen-turbo-handel-/7855286.html

Welchering, P. (2012, November 2012). *www.faz.net*. Retrieved December 7, 2017, from http://www.faz.net/aktuell/technik-motor/digital/hochfrequenzhandel-der-turbo-algorithmus-im-boersennetz-11972699-p3.html

World Economy, E. &. (Ed.). (2014, August 26). *www.weed-online.org*. Retrieved December 3, 2017, from http://www.weed-online.org/show/7849062.html?searchshow=high%20frequency%20trading

www.bafin.de. (2014, January 31). Retrieved 2017, from https://www.bafin.de/EN/Aufsicht/BoersenMaerkte/Hochfrequenzhandel/high_frequency_trading_node_en.html

www.investopedia.com. (n.d.). Retrieved December 8, 2017, from https://www.investopedia.com/terms/q/quote-stuffing.asp

www.nanex.net. (2013, July 22). Retrieved December 8, 2017, from http://www.nanex.net/aqck2/4371.html

www.nasdaqomx.com. (n.d.). Retrieved December 6, 2017, from http://www.nasdaqomx.com/transactions/connectivity-services/nordic-sponsored-access

www.wikipedia.org. (n.d.). Retrieved December 3, 2017, from https://en.wikipedia.org/wiki/Algorithmic_trading

YOUR KNOWLEDGE HAS VALUE

- We will publish your bachelor's and master's thesis, essays and papers

- Your own eBook and book - sold worldwide in all relevant shops

- Earn money with each sale

Upload your text at www.GRIN.com and publish for free